# UNDERSTANDING HUMAN DESIGN CENTERS

UNCOVER THE UNIQUENESS WITHIN YOUR ENERGETIC BLUEPRINT

LISA FERNANDES

FOREWORD BY
AMY ELIZABETH

Copyright © 2022 by Lisa Fernandes

All rights reserved.

No part of this book may be reproduced in any form or by any electronic or mechanical means, including information storage and retrieval systems, without written permission from the author, except for the use of brief quotations in a book review.

# CONTENTS

Dedication — v
Foreword — vii
A Gift For You — xi

1. Introduction — 1
2. The 101 — 4
3. Your Chart — 13
4. The Initiator — 15
5. The Analyst — 23
6. The Expressor — 31
7. The Magnet — 39
8. Unlearn, Adapt, Relearn — 46
9. The Go-Getter — 51
10. The Feeler — 59
11. The Ignitor — 67
12. The Whisperer — 75
13. The Caffeinator — 83
14. Unfolding — 91

Resources — 95

# DEDICATION

To my babies, Noah and Leo. I love you.

— MOMMY

# FOREWORD

Foreward by Amy Elizabeth, *Align by Design HD*

---

It has been a pleasure and honor to know Lisa since 2018. Her joy and ability to connect with others in a human way is admirable. I've witnessed Lisa align with her design, utilize her passion for creativity, and live outside any boxes that feel inauthentic.

She has stood in her womanhood while integrating Human Design, as she became a mother of two and shifted her life. Lisa is one of the most intuitive, and intelligent women, with the world now ready to hear and feel her. She is a true inspiration to many.

Throughout her own personal work and the work within Human Design, she became Certified in Human Design through Align by Design and brought it to life in her own signature. It has been the most beautiful story she has written in real time for herself, and of course, the impact is felt from others, as it will within this book.

---

The centers within Human Design are essential to not just personal power, but also the ability to understand the parts of us that are not truly ours. As we align within our design, we begin to feel the truth of ourselves and our authenticity becomes loud - our drive, our passion, our excitement, our designs, our energy, and yes, our emotions. Each of these unique parts are housed within the body as Human Design centers.

Anything that feels forced, confusing or anxious comes from the centers that are undefined in our body graph. This can be confusing before and during alignment as we don't understand the anxiety and confusion. It becomes so clear, powerful and life changing when we do understand the potency, confidence and ability to trust ourselves through knowing how to work these undefined centers, and where to focus our energy.

---

The journey of the Human Design centers can not be replaced — much conditioning comes through personal experiences and personal desires. This is the beauty of the journey, it's *UNIQUE*.

Throughout this incredible resource, that Lisa has creatively and intelligently provided, you will finally, now, not only feel the power in your uniqueness but GET it. You will have certainty and clarity in knowing YOU and everything that isn't you.

The perfect combination of intuition and intelligence.

Enjoy.

— *Amy Elizabeth*, *Founder of Align by Design HD*

**A Gift To Amplify Your Human Design Journey:**

*3 SECRETS OF MANIFESTATION USING HUMAN DESIGN*

**VISIT THE LINK/QR:**

https://bit.ly/HDmanifestationsecrets

# CHAPTER 1
# INTRODUCTION

As humans, we make moves every minute of everyday. Physical moves. Energetic moves. Emotional moves. Sometimes we overthink, and other times we make a move so fast, we swore all we did, was blink.

For the majority of my life, I've thought twice about everything. I felt very little freedom, until one moment. Let me explain…

### JANUARY 2018

I walked across the creaky boards of the porch to reach an open door. I stepped inside the sunroom. I remember the faint smell of frankinsense as my heart raced. I looked up to a face asking, "What can I help you with?"

"I don't know" I replied.

. . .

Moments later, I was sobbing.

I was in the midst of a rock-bottom. I stood there with tears streaming down my face and felt empty, lost, and misunderstood. To be honest, I questioned everything (including taking my own life).

## 2 WEEKS LATER...

My phone dinged. I looked down to a notification from Instagram. An account was going live, I clicked and joined.

The livestream would change the way I viewed myself and the way I would now move through life. All I had to do was click a button.

Once the livestream ended, I sent a message, received a link and paid for a program about Human Design — all within a moment.

My body buzzed, a temporary high of euphoria.

And that's when things changed.

---

My name is Lisa and I've created *Understanding the Human Design Centers*. A resource to illuminate the powerful tools within your energetic blueprint. The energetic blueprint being your Human Design.

Since finding Human Design in 2018, my life has *radically* changed. I sit here now, writing this book so you, too, can have the same opportunity. I am writing so you can not only learn about yourself and your loved ones but deeply understand them. I desire for you to have more compassion, connection and by default, expand your capacity to grow deeper relationships.

Inside this book you will learn about how your centers within Human Design can provide permission to be you, in all of your uniqueness. You'll see how they uncover your tendencies, your strengths and allow you to see the space in-between. The dark space where you may have once believed was a downfall, is actually the spark waiting to ignite your potentiality.

Human Design unlocked something special within me and maybe, now, you'll find it too.

# CHAPTER 2
# THE 101

*"Never memorize anything you can look up."*

ALBERT EINSTEIN

Human Design can be a little complex. When I bought my first Human Design book, I opened it up and my mind immediately bounced between two things: WHAT!? and _____ (blank). As you can imagine, the excitement I once had, now looked a bit grim. I put the book away and it continues to collect dust in a corner somewhere.

Don't worry, I won't put you through the same torture. Inside this book, you will find applicable and comprehensible information. And though I don't fancy teaching the "bones" Human Design is created from, I appreciate the curiosity so I'll cover the basics.

The Human Design bodygraph is created by bringing together many different modalities:

- Astrology
- The I'ching
- Chakras
- Tree of Life
- Quantum Mechanics
- Astronomy
- Genetics
- Biochemistry

To find your Human Design, you can access a free chart on many different sites - I personally love mybodygraph.com.

In order to create a chart, you require three key pieces of information:

- Date of birth
- Exact time of birth
- Location of birth

For those reading who do not have your access to your exact time of birth, my suggestion would be to call the hospital you were born and request medical records. The birth time is important and I don't ever suggest "guessing" as it could result in aligning with an incorrect energy type and that, my friends, defeats the purpose.

When you look at a bodygraph aka your "chart", it is composed of shapes – triangles, squares and a diamond. These shapes are the centers within Human Design. These centers allow energy to go in and out of the body, each serving a specific function.

The centers in Human Design originate from the traditional chakra system, comprised of 7 chakras.

*the 7-chakra system*

In Human Design, there are 9 centers. In order to create the 9 centers, the energy from the 7-chakra system split within two chakras. The heart chakra splits to create the g and heart center and the solar plexus chakra splits into the solar plexus and spleen center.

*the heart chakra splitting, to create the g and heart centers in Human Design*

The Nine Centers within Human Design are:

- Head
- Ajna
- Throat
- G
- Heart
- Solar Plexus
- Sacral
- Spleen
- Root

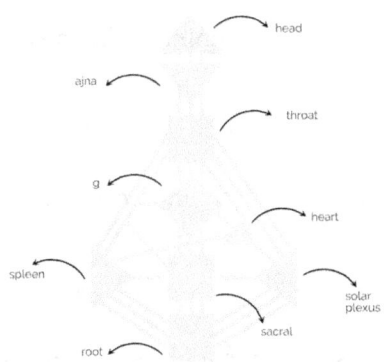

*the location of the 9 centers in Human Design*

Within these nine centers there are awareness, motor, pressure, identity and expression centers.

## A QUICK REFERENCE BY CENTER:

The *head* center is a pressure center and is a center for ideas and inspiration.

The *ajna* center is an awareness center and is a center for conceptualization and analysis.

The *throat* is a center for expression and is used for manifestation and communication.

The *g* center is an identity center and is a center for love and direction.

The *heart* is a motor center and is the center for ego and willpower.

The *solar plexus* is a motor and awareness center and is the home to our emotions.

The *sacral* center is a motor and is our life force energy.

The *spleen* is an awareness center and allows us to tap into our intuition.

The *root* is a pressure and motor center and is for stress and adrenaline.

## THE NOT-SELF THEME

When an individual is in a low expression of a center, they commonly feel their not-self theme. The not-self is the quickest way for us to know when we are not in alignment — it is our indicator change needs to occur.

**Not-Self Themes by Design Type:**

- Generators: *Frustration*
- Manifesting Generators: *Frustration*
- Manifestors: *Anger*
- Projectors: *Bitterness*
- Reflectors: *Disappointment*

## DEFINED VS. UNDEFINED

In addition to the center's function, the center will be defined or undefined. The defined centers will be colored in and the undefined centers will be white.

Our defined centers hold and transmit the energy we put into the world. This energy can be seen and felt within our Aura and when in alignment, is consistent and reliable. The consistency of this energy can feel secure which can create a more concrete knowing of who we are.

Our undefined centers are energy we take in from others. These undefined centers do not have access to consistent energy which can lead to a natural attraction to a center defined in another persons bodygraph. For example: If I have an undefined g center, I will naturally be attracted to someone with a defined g. Their strong and consistent sense of identity attracts me to them.

Both defined and undefined centers will have conditioning (also known as a shadow frequency). The defined conditioning looks more like "I'm too much" whereas the undefined conditioning looks like, "I'm not enough". Though both have conditioning, the undefined centers are prone to more — they often take on feelings, thoughts and ideas of the other. All that is taken into the undefined center is for the greater good. When used correctly, it can turn into wisdom.

## WRAPPING UP

Ok, I'm going to provide a quick "coles notes" before diving into the particulars. I understand some material goes over our head and it can be challenging to know which information is important to remember so:

# UNDERSTANDING HUMAN DESIGN CENTERS

**Defined**

- Consistent energy
- What we give to others
- Internal pressure
- Appear colored within the bodygraph

*defined centers are colored in the bodygraph*

**Undefined**

- Inconsistent energy
- What we receive from others
- External pressure
- Appear white within your bodygraph

*undefined centers are white in the bodygraph*

. . .

Someone with an undefined center can be attracted to those with the opposite definition, a defined center.

In the next few chapters you will learn about each center in the defined and undefined expressions. It's time to utilize the strengths inside these powerful spaces within us, let's gooooo.

# CHAPTER 3
# YOUR CHART

*on the following page, use the blank chart to identify your defined and undefined centers*

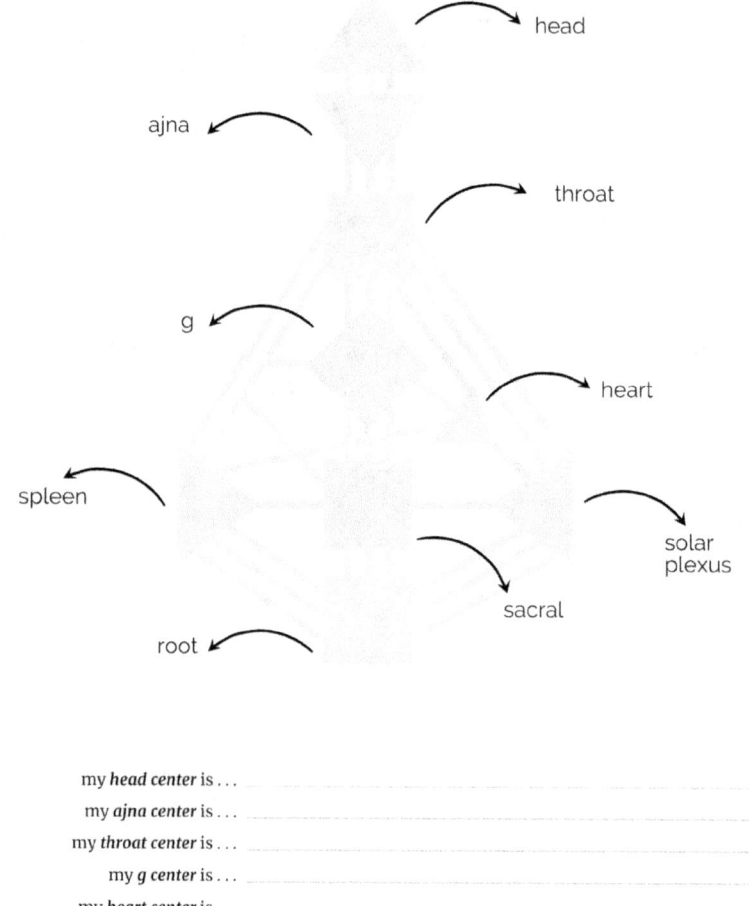

my *head center* is . . .
my *ajna center* is . . .
my *throat center* is . . .
my *g center* is . . .
my *heart center* is . . .
my *solar plexus center* is . . .
my *sacral center* is . . .
my *spleen center* is . . .
my *root center* is . . .

## CHAPTER 4
## THE INITIATOR

The initiator aka the head center, is the top triangle within the bodygraph. The *head* is a pressure center and is a center for ideas and inspiration.

### THE DEFINED HEAD

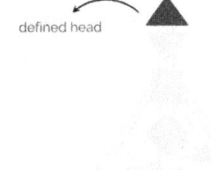
defined head

30% of the population have a defined head.

The defined head creates a consistent and reliable source of inspiration and ideas. When following your strategy and authority, you will create impact and motivation to inspire those around you. With a defined head, it is important to understand that timing is the key to utilizing the center appropriately. When you release the pressure of acting on *all* your ideas, you are able to maximize your potential - this takes patience and practice.

Spoiler alert, following your strategy and authority will guide you to know when to act on ideas and inspiration.

---

*"Inspiration is already within me."*

AFFIRMATION FOR THE DEFINED HEAD

---

Low expression of the defined head can look like:

- You find it hard to change your opinion once you've made up your mind (it's your idea and you want to keep it)
- You may feel hopeless due to the pressure to act on ideas
- Always trying to figure things out, even when they do not relate to you
- Forcing, interrupting, seeking attention
- Not sharing your thoughts and inspirations due to fear

High expression of the defined head can look like:

- Clear mental process in relation to your own inspiration/ideas
- Awareness to find answers when appropriate
- You trust that in time, the right answers will find you
- You hold strong boundaries
- You lead powerful conversations
- You are highly inspirational

## AN EXAMPLE OF LIVING WITH A DEFINED HEAD

Stefan has a defined head. For as long as he can remember he has been inquisitive — always asking questions. As he transitioned into adulthood, he noticed that many people would express frustration when he continually asking questions. The frustration confused Stefan as he didn't understand why it seemed no one cared.

During a conversation with his sister-in-law, she asked "do you have a defined head"? Stefan had no idea what she was talking about and asked her to explain. As he asked questions about Human Design, Stefan quickly realized many people in his family have an undefined 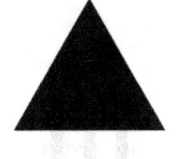 head. He understands now that asking questions to someone with an undefined head can not only cause them frustration but can cause them to feel uncertain and undervalued.

## THE UNDEFINED HEAD

70% of the population have an undefined head.

With an undefined head, your access to inspiration comes from outside of you — being inspired by environments, events or people. The inconsistent flow of inspiration and ideas can cause pressure to answer questions and find solutions, when in reality you are here to ask questions and allow solutions to flow to you. The function of the head is not to find answers, it is here for ideas, inspiration and be open to possibility. So, even though there is pressure to find answers, the key for the undefined head is patience.

Another common theme with the undefined head center, is feeling pressure in the form of avoidance or over-consuming. You may avoid due to a stream of information coming into the head or over-consume, feeling you "need" to learn in order to understand.

. . .

A great tool for the undefined head center is to find a quiet space, detach from time and truly observe and surrender to your thoughts.

---

*"Inspiration flows to me"*

AFFIRMATION FOR THE UNDEFINED HEAD

---

Low expression of the undefined head can look like:

- Thinking about irrelevant matters
- Being impatient
- You try to answer everyone's questions and forget about your own
- Getting caught up in feeling you "need" to stay busy
- Going in circles not getting anything done
- Forcing ideas and inspiration

High expression of the undefined head can look like:

- You can sense another person's thoughts and ideas
- Exploring thoughts freely and without attachment
- Ability to surrender and trust that inspiration will find you
- Heightened awareness when to tune-in or to stop consuming

- Accepting that not all issues are your problem to solve

## AN EXAMPLE OF LIVING WITH AN UNDEFINED HEAD

Maxine has an undefined head. A constant battle for Maxine is the constant search for answers. Maxine is unable to focus on one task, moves from topic to topic and never completes a project. Maxine is a business owner and finds herself enrolled in program, feeling she will never know enough.

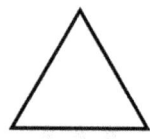

When Maxine learns about Human Design and discovers the wisdom of the undefined head, she begins to practice non-attachment - Maxine starts to recognize thoughts and ideas coming in and out of the head. When Maxine feels overwhelmed, she goes for a walk to allow space for clarity. Maxine's awareness of the undefined head begins to allow her to filter thoughts and inspirations with more ease while releasing pressure to find answers to everything.

**DEFINED HEAD**
*notes, reflections, people I know with a defined head*

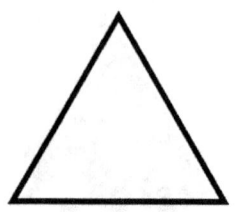

**UNDEFINED HEAD**

*notes, reflections, people I know with an undefined head*

# CHAPTER 5
# THE ANALYST

The analyst aka the ajna, is the second triangle from the top of the bodygraph. The *ajna* center is an awareness center and is a center for conceptualization and analysis.

## THE DEFINED AJNA

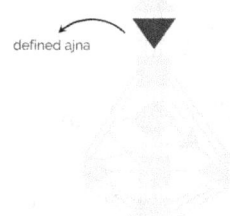

47% of the population have a defined ajna.

. . .

With a defined ajna, you have a consistent way of thinking and filtering information. The specific way the defined ajna conceptualizes, creates great certainty in how they communicate, present information and act within the world. When information comes into your awareness, the defined ajna will hold onto it, causing a feeling of overwhelm or over-stimulation.

When there is something to learn, you are able to organize your thoughts in a set pattern. At times, this may cause you to deter an opinion or viewpoint, especially if it differs from your own. A great practice is to always follow your strategy and authority before sharing.

*"My active mind creates efficiency for myself and others."*

AFFIRMATION FOR THE DEFINED AJNA

Low expression of the defined ajna can look like:

- You are defensive when someone doesn't agree with you
- You may find yourself stuck in your way of thinking so you force your ideas onto others
- Unable to accept other points of view, a "my way or the highway" mentality

High expression of the defined ajna can look like:

- Ability to soothe doubt others are experiencing
- You trust the way you build opinions
- You research before expressing to the world
- Actively listen to the voice of others without shutting them down

## AN EXAMPLE OF LIVING WITH A DEFINED AJNA

Ana has a defined ajna and most people call Ana stubborn. She is always one to argue and disagree at the dinner table which makes people uncomfortable. Ana's friend Joe mentioned Human Design to her and although it took her months of convincing, she finally looked into it. When Ana learned about the defined ajna she became deeply aware of all the times she didn't listen to the opinions of her friends. This awareness has allowed her to no longer force her opinion, and be open to new ideas.

## THE UNDEFINED AJNA

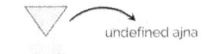
undefined ajna

53% of the population have an undefined ajna.

Having an undefined ajna means you have an open and fluid mind, it is not meant for certainty. The undefined ajna receives information and ideas from all around. Being undefined in this center, you are absorbing constantly within your environment and awareness, taking in bits and pieces and subsequently turning it into wisdom. You have the ability to take in what matters to you and leave the rest - a beautiful life skill.

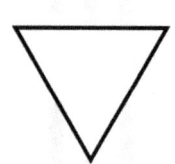

A quick note: you are not here to "know everything", you are here to ask for clarity and enjoy new ideas and thoughts fluidly.

At times you may find you are absent-minded and distracted as information freely moves through the ajna. If it feels good for you, a helpful tip is to keep a calendar or journal to stay organized.

"My ability to remain open is a gift for the collective."

AFFIRMATION FOR THE UNDEFINED AJNA

Low expression of the undefined ajna can look like:

- Feeling confused so you pretend to understand
- You may feel stress or anxiety about sharing your opinion/response to a question
- No fixed way of thinking which can cause confusion
- You may feel the "need" to be right and find answers through overcompensating by talking too much

High expression of the undefined ajna can look like:

- You feel secure in your way of thinking
- You feel comfortable asking for clarity without the need to be correct
- You do not need reassurance, you understand that not having a fixed way of thinking allows you to think in ways others aren't able to
- You understand you do not need certainty in order to take action.
- Your opinion is valued

## AN EXAMPLE OF LIVING WITH AN UNDEFINED AJNA

Jason has an undefined ajna. He is very open-minded, with no consistent desire to learn about certain topics. Jason arrives at a work party where he finds himself at a table where everyone is talking politics. Jason knows very little about politics so he begins to feel stressed he could be asked his opinion because he knows he's going to do what he always does - pretend to know what he's talking about. The work party ends and he has managed to dodge any questions

- pewf. He has lunch with a friend who shares about what it means to have an undefined ajna, he discovers this applies to him and now understands that he can engage in conversations by being inquisitive and actively listening.

**DEFINED AJNA**
*notes, reflections, people I know with a defined ajna*

___

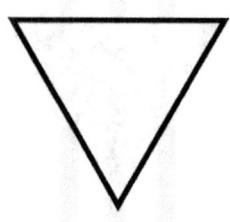

UNDEFINED AJNA

*notes, reflections, people I know with an undefined ajna*

# CHAPTER 6
# THE EXPRESSOR

The expressor aka the throat center, is the first square within the bodygraph. The *throat* is a center for expression and is used for manifestation and communication.

## THE DEFINED THROAT

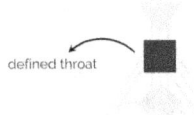

72% of the population have a defined throat.

· · ·

With a defined throat you have access to consistent communication. You are able to articulate with confidence, some may even call you a natural leader. When following your strategy and authority, your words can be both powerful and motivational. However, when used incorrectly, the impact is lost and can even deter people.

With a defined throat, an important and efficient use of this center is to only speak from a place of truth and desire.

---

*"When I communication my desires, the universe responds."*

AFFIRMATION FOR THE DEFINED THROAT

---

Low expression of the defined throat can look like:

- You find it difficult when you are interrupted so you interrupt others
- You lose impact from over-speaking
- You do not express yourself
- People feel you're too much
- Unable to trust what you have to say matters

# UNDERSTANDING HUMAN DESIGN CENTERS    33

High expression of the defined throat can look like:

- Confident and empowered voice
- You trust your expression
- You speak clearly with no expectation or pressure placed on the impact
- There is no pressure to speak, you understand to trust the timing of your expression

## AN EXAMPLE OF LIVING WITH A DEFINED THROAT

Jenna is a news broadcaster. Her voice on screen is captivating, she is a natural at her job and she loves it - this is Jenna's high expression of the defined throat. When Jenna is off-screen, her confidence wavers.

When she feels uninspired or under pressure, she doesn't express herself or finds herself angry when people don't agree with what she has to say - the low expression of the defined throat. The low expression can occur when not following your strategy and authority.

## THE UNDEFINED THROAT

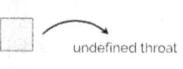

28% of the population have an undefined throat.

With an undefined throat, you are here to be wise with your expression. Those with undefined throats are excellent advocates for the voice of the other and can express this through speaking or other modes of communication such as writing. A gift of the undefined throat is to gain wisdom through listening, absorbing and then bringing your teachings to the world. The inconsistency of the throat center can cause pressure to speak so being aware of this is important.

When utilizing this center, be sure to follow your strategy and authority.

---

*"My expression is a vessel for others."*

AFFIRMATION FOR THE UNDEFINED THROAT

Low expression of the undefined throat can look like:

- You feel nervous speaking
- You may feel uncomfortable with silence and feel the need to speak even when it's not appropriate
- You may feel ignored and that your opinion is not valued
- You overthink what you should express and speak seldom

High expression of the undefined throat can look like:

- You have many ways of expressing yourself
- You do not feel pressure to speak
- You hold faith that your strategy and authority will guide you to speak from desire for yourself and the collective.

## AN EXAMPLE OF LIVING WITH AN UNDEFINED THROAT

Maverick has an undefined throat and finds it difficult to express himself around his friend, Georgia. When Maverick is in larger groups, he has no problem communicating - Maverick is able to adapt to the conversation but not when Georgia is present.

Soon after, Maverick and Georgia find out they both have undefined throats. They have found it difficult to compute around one another due to their lack of awareness and consistency in their throat center. When they are in groups,

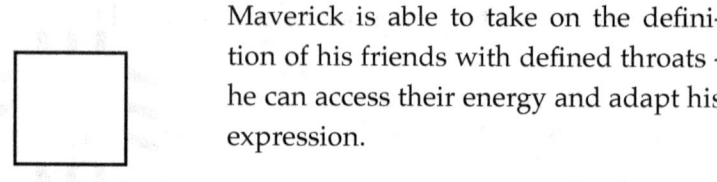 Maverick is able to take on the definition of his friends with defined throats - he can access their energy and adapt his expression.

# UNDERSTANDING HUMAN DESIGN CENTERS

**DEFINED THROAT**
*notes, reflections, people I know with a defined throat*

**UNDEFINED THROAT**

*notes, reflections, people I know with an undefined throat*

# CHAPTER 7
# THE MAGNET

The magnet aka the g center, is the diamond located in the middle of the bodygraph. The *g* center is an identity center and is the center for love and direction.

## THE DEFINED G

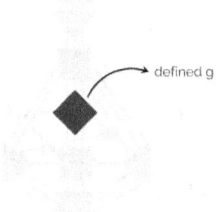

57% of the population have a defined g

With a defined g center you are a strong source of love and direction for others and you, yourself, have a strong internal

 compass that guides your identity. When following your strategy and authority, you will trust in following your path, even when it feels unsteady. With such a clear direction for your own life, you may find you can provide guidance for others as well. It will be important for you to have energetic boundaries as your defined g is a natural attractor to those with an undefined g center.

*"Each step I take brings me closer to where I am meant to be."*

AFFIRMATION FOR THE DEFINED G

Low expression of the defined g can look like:

- Fear of being an outcast due to the certainty of your path
- You may have a lack of confidence in yourself
- You may focus too much on other people's journeys instead of your own
- You may not accept the identity chosen by people around you and attempt to convince them otherwise

High expression of the defined g can look like:

- You model identity for those with an undefined g
- Able to express and receive love in a stable way
- You are able to move through life with clarity moment-to-moment
- You surrender to love, life and express freely
- You honor the path of others

## AN EXAMPLE OF LIVING WITH A DEFINED G

Gill works at a law firm in London, England. Ever since she was in grade-school she knew she wanted to work in a court room and joked about living overseas. Gill grew up in a small town in Missouri and even though many of her friends never left home, she was determined to leave. When she moved to England many people reached out to her on Facebook asking how she did it. Though Gill can come off arrogant at times, she always tries to have compassion for those in her life, knowing not everyone has so much certainty as she does.

## THE UNDEFINED G

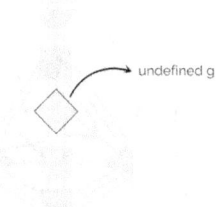

43% of the population have an undefined g center.

With an undefined g center, your identity is not fixed, some may even call you a chameleon. You ebb and flow though life, embracing new careers and new desires. You are meant to move through life sampling people, places and feelings to see what is right for you.

Your biggest strength will be trusting your strategy and authority. Enjoy the ride and allow your desires to drive you. When you do this, you'll quickly know what is for you or what is not for you.

---

*"I am mindful of who I spend my time with. I understand my openness will be drawn to the identity of another"*

AFFIRMATION FOR THE UNDEFINED G

---

Low expression of the undefined g can look like:

- You may find yourself forcing an identity that does not belong to you
- You are constantly searching for love and direction
- You attach yourself to people and locations in order to feel safe
- You can feel lost and out of place

# UNDERSTANDING HUMAN DESIGN CENTERS

High expression of the undefined g can look like:

- You surrender to life
- You understand your identity will change in different phases of life
- You are detached from the need to stay in one place and allow yourself to freely move though life
- You see which people and places are for you and trust when to pivot and move
- You provide comfort to others who feel lost

## AN EXAMPLE OF LIVING WITH AN UNDEFINED G

Fabio's family is worried about him. The family is worried because Fabio is 36 and has not been in a job for more than a year.

Fabio is an artist — he has worked many positions over the years including freelancing graffiti, front desk at an art museum, stand up comedy, a bartender and most recently, abstract painting. At times, Fabio feels uneasy leaving a job to move onto something new but he 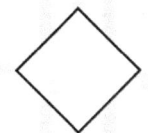 always knows it's the right thing to do. The continued trust Fabio holds allows him to have more happiness and ease in job transitioning.

**DEFINED G**

*notes, reflections, people I know with a defined g*

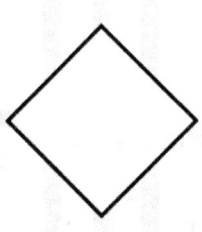

**UNDEFINED G**
*notes, reflections, people I know with an undefined g*

## CHAPTER 8
## UNLEARN, ADAPT, RELEARN

> There's so much emphasis on "it's ok to not be ok." We often need to hear: "it's ok to feel good, even if other people do not."
>
> THE HOLISTIC PSYCHOLOGIST

A lot of coaches and healers in the Human Design space will talk about the Human Design Experiment. You may be asking, "WTF does that even mean?"

To me, there are three phases of the Human Design experiment: information, integration and embodiment. The over-arching theme of anyone's experiment is to unlearn, adapt and relearn new ways of being.

. . .

During the information phase, you take in knowledge and learning at a rate that feels comfortable. Many people spend too much time here - taking in mountains of information and finding themselves going nowhere fast = no change or results.

Information overload can send us into a spiral, not knowing where to focus energy. If you find yourself here, I encourage taking a step back and asking, "what is going well?" and "what can I change today?" A barrier to evolving within your experiment is feeling powerless. When we are overwhelmed and unable to focus, we give away power. By asking yourself what is going well, you reinforce positive change. By asking yourself what can I change today? You enable a chance to pivot or zero-in on patterns in order to recognize a pattern to shift it.

This leads us into the next step, integration.

The integration phase of the experiment is when we take our learning and begin to create change. You may find yourself trying to recognize patterns and ways of being in an effort to apply of "integrate" your learning.

During integration, your heightened awareness allows you to unlearning old behaviours. You can then give yourself permission to adapt and relearning new ways of being. Spoiler: this stage can be a bit exhausting as our brain uses more energy while on high-alert.

. . .

As you become more energetically aligned it can feel good. (It can always feeling "yuck" - more on this below).

We have been wired as a collective to make others happy, to adapt our life to accommodate for family, colleagues and sometimes, to even put ourself last. A very unsustainable model, if you ask me. When you begin to altar your patterns, the people around you will be affected whether we desire it or not. You may find, people become disappointed, frustrated, angry. Projected emotions can make us feel guilt and tempt us to go back to old behaviour that does not serve us.

Notice where you allow guilt to take the place of positive emotions and know this:

*It is ok to say no.*
*It is ok to step away from unhealthy relationships.*
*You are worthy of better love.*
*You have nothing to prove.*
*It is okay to walk away.*

Next up, the embodiment phase. The embodiment phase of the Human Design experiment takes time. It occurs when alignment comes naturally, you consciously make decisions and actions that support your energetic blueprint. I could go in-depth on embodiment but I do not believe it would serve for the purpose of this book.

. . .

# UNDERSTANDING HUMAN DESIGN CENTERS 49

As we dive into the last five centers, continue to extend compassion to yourself. In the low expression of a center? Incredible (*no, seriously*). It's what we're here for and why I wrote this book - for us to all unlearn, adapt and relearn.

I've always had an innate willingness to help others which as you can imagine, this showcased my low expression *often* as I became aware of my Human Design. It has allowed me to showcase my wisdom, grow stronger relationships and be here today.

If you've read this far, you desire to help people. My mission is to reach as many souls as possible to bring clarity and awareness to their lives. In order to do this, I need your help. In todays world, our voices matter. I would be forever grateful for 60 seconds of your time to review this book on Amazon. Reviewing allows others to build trust in me, leading to more eyes, hearts and souls touched.

From one soul to another, thank you for taking the time to review. Your support means more than you know.

. . .

Let's jump back in.

# CHAPTER 9
# THE GO-GETTER

The heart is the smaller triangle shape on the right side of the bodygraph. The *heart* is a motor center and is the center for ego and willpower.

## THE DEFINED HEART

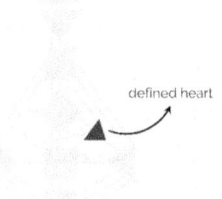

37% of the population have a defined heart.

With a defined heart you have access to consistent willpower. When following your strategy and authority, you can have a balance of work and flow which stems from your ability to see your own value and worth. You enjoy having control over your life in all aspects - work, life, love.

With a defined heart, only say yes to tasks by following your strategy and authority - when you don't, you will find it difficult to complete the task or find it falls flat. If it's right, you can go, go, go, till it's done.

---

*"My consistency fuels my soul."*

### AFFIRMATION FOR THE DEFINED HEART

---

Low expression of the defined heart can look like:

- You may appear arrogant, over confident, selfish
- You feel you have something to prove and find yourself wanting to win, just to win
- You may overspend, overwork and project upon others
- You hold weak boundaries around events and/or work you schedule for yourself

# UNDERSTANDING HUMAN DESIGN CENTERS

High expression of the defined heart can look like:

- You empower others
- You are in love with your work
- You are competitive in a healthy way
- You enjoy challenging yourself to do more and be better on a deep level

## AN EXAMPLE OF LIVING WITH A DEFINED HEART

Julien thrives with a consistent schedule. He enjoys the reliability of his 6am work-outs, his 9-5 schedule and family time in the evening. On Friday night's he has the neighbours over for game-night. He has been called a "sore-loser" a couple times when he's not on the winning team but most of the time, Julien is a good-sport and is in it for the fun of the game.

## THE UNDEFINED HEART

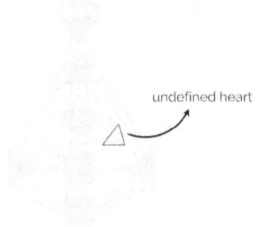

63% of the population have an undefined heart.

When your heart is undefined, your willpower and feeling of worthiness is not consistent. This inconsistency may make you feel as though you have something to prove - the opposite is true. Remove the idea and expectation that you have to show up consistently everyday as this does not reflect your capability. You are designed to show up in a way that feels good for you, this is how you shine. Think of it this way — you create your own lane. Consider this your permission slip — you do not have to work or show up like others do because your way is best for your divine path.

---

*"No matter the circumstances, I am worthy. No exceptions. I am worthy no matter what."*

AFFIRMATION FOR THE UNDEFINED HEART

---

Low expression of the undefined heart can look like:

- You may feel powerless, as though you don't bring value
- Can feel a low sense of self worth so you may try to prove your worth
- You may make commitments from a place of ego
- You say yes to things without desire

High expression of the undefined heart can look like:

- You are sensitive to power struggles and are compassionate to others
- You do not make promises
- You deeply understand that you have nothing to prove
- You allow yourself to move through life at your own pace

## AN EXAMPLE OF LIVING WITH AN UNDEFINED HEART:

Darren is a freelancer, he creates his own hours and has the opportunity to travel for work. Once a quarter, he is asked to go into NYC to lead a videographer training which involves two weeks of 10am-6pm work days. He describes these two weeks as "torture" and tells to his friend he feels trapped every time he goes to NYC.

Darren's friend has been around for years and just "gets" how Darren is likely feeling. He has witnessed Darren ebb and flow with his schedule. Some days not starting work till 11am and still getting done before heading to the gym at 2pm. Darren's friend suggests during his time in NYC, he switch up the daily schedule - after all, he's the one leading it. Darren huffs and puffs and then states, "why don't I just say no?"

. . .

Turns out, the quarterly training isn't mandatory. Next quarter, Darren says no. The quarter after, he feels ready to jump back in and try things his way.

# UNDERSTANDING HUMAN DESIGN CENTERS

**DEFINED HEART**
*notes, reflections, people I know with a defined heart*

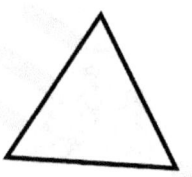

**UNDEFINED HEART**
*notes, reflections, people I know with an undefined heart*

# CHAPTER 10
# THE FEELER

The feeler aka the solar plexus, is the triangle located on the right side of the bodygraph. The *solar plexus* is a motor and awareness center and is the home to our emotions.

## THE DEFINED SOLAR PLEXUS

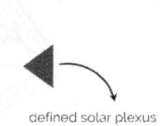
defined solar plexus

53% of the population have a defined solar plexus.

. . .

Someone with a defined solar plexus can be described as someone who feels it all. If you have this center defined, the solar plexus is your inner authority. Emotionally, it is your nature to experience a spectrum of feelings - the ups, the downs and the in-between. When the defined solar plexus feels emotional highs and lows, they are a chemical response within the body. Knowing this, a great practice is to detach from feelings. Allow yourself to go through emotions with awareness and compassion for the self, knowing there is nothing you have done to create this feeling.

While you are moving through a wave of emotion, you may notice your feelings rub off on others because, well, they do. In these moments, removing yourself from the environment, even if it means excusing yourself for five minutes, can be a powerful tool to exercise.

---

*"I am meant to feel emotions. I allow myself to use my emotional energy to express into the world. The more I allow, the faster the feeling will pass."*

AFFIRMATION FOR THE DEFINED SOLAR PLEXUS

---

Low expression of the defined solar plexus can look like:

- Can feel intense to others and drive them away

- You may find yourself impatient during an emotional high, leading to making decisions before reaching a state of calm / clarity
- You don't allow yourself time to settle into new environments
- You project your discomfort of emotions onto others

High expression of the defined solar plexus can look like:

- You are comfortable with the full range of human emotions
- You trust and surrender into your capacity to feel
- You understand you need more time to make decisions
- You do not make decisions when in emotional highs or lows
- You do not rush

## AN EXAMPLE OF LIVING WITH A DEFINED SOLAR PLEXUS

Leo has a defined solar plexus. On Friday night, Leo's wife asked about moving to Arizona. Leo was hit by a wave of emotions, he immediately reacted to the question with frustration. They argued for over an hour about how it wasn't the right time, it was too much work and not having the resources to re-locate. That night, Leo didn't sleep — he lay awake thinking about moving and the next day, still felt uneasy. It wasn't until later in the evening Leo was able to speak to his wife and have a conversation about the possibility to move.

Leo, like many other emotionally defined individuals, was filled with emotion when faced with a difficult question. Once time had passed to allow the emotional wave to pass, he energetically arrived in a space of clarity to speak.

## THE UNDEFINED SOLAR PLEXUS

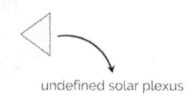
undefined solar plexus

47% of the population have an undefined solar plexus.

With an undefined solar plexus, your natural state is calm and collected. When around others, the undefined solar plexus will take-in the emotions. Your reality with an undefined solar plexus is many emotions are projected your way (almost) constantly which can make you a powerful empath but this can also create a state of overwhelm. Though you are feeling emotions frequently, you are not meant to hold them, they are meant to flow in and out of your energetic body. In order to release the emotions of another person, you must first recognize they are not your own.

. . .

When emotions arise, ask yourself — do these emotions belong to me? If they aren't your own, allow yourself to energetically detach and release.

*"I allow myself to release emotions that are not mine."*

## AFFIRMATION FOR THE UNDEFINED SOLAR PLEXUS

Low expression of the undefined solar plexus can look like:

- Unable to process and filter emotions
- You may be unable to differentiate where emotions are coming from
- You may feel completely cut off from emotions (unable to feel)
- You feel in a state of overwhelm (from feeling too much)

High expression of the undefined solar plexus can look like:

- You are able to recognize emotions that belong to you and which do not
- You allow yourself to release the emotions of the other people
- You are deeply empathetic and compassionate

## AN EXAMPLE OF LIVING WITH AN UNDEFINED SOLAR PLEXUS

Patel has an undefined solar plexus. Patel works full-time as a new nurse. On her days away from the hospital she does yoga, reads and has an active social life. Over the years, she becomes sensitive to others. When she is at work, she experiences a range of feelings from sadness, to fear, to anger, to disappointment. Over the years, she felt herself shutting down — she builds up walls, causing her to no longer feel emotion at all.

She feels helpless. A friend recommends Patel to try reiki so she books a session. Once the session is complete, the practitioner explains she is experiencing heaviness in her solar plexus, a common trait for someone with an undefined solar plexus within Human Design. Patel and the reiki practitioner discuss healthy ways to clear the solar plexus as well as non-attachment practices.

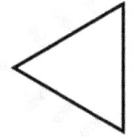

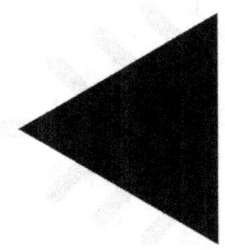

DEFINED SOLAR PLEXUS
*notes, reflections, people I know with a defined solar plexus*

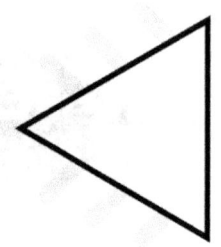

**UNDEFINED SOLAR PLEXUS**
*notes, reflections, people I know with an undefined solar plexus*

_____
_____
_____
_____
_____
_____
_____
_____
_____
_____
_____
_____
_____
_____
_____
_____
_____
_____
_____
_____
_____
_____
_____

# CHAPTER 11
# THE IGNITOR

T he ignitor aka the sacral center, is the second last square within the bodygraph. The *sacral* center is a motor and is our life force energy.

## THE DEFINED SACRAL

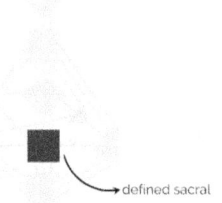
defined sacral

66% of the population have a defined sacral.

The sacral center houses our life force energy and is one of the most powerful motors within the Human Design bodygraph.

The sacral is activated by truth and desire and is known for its clarity. When asked a question - your sacral will show you a clear yes or no. This is black and white - there is no gray area. With a defined sacral, your desires fuel you. Meaning, desires ignite the sacral motor to provide more energy. The energy produced from this center may create a desire to "go", though it's important to remember that as a sacral being, you are not here to initiate, you respond. Since not everyone has a defined sacral, those who are undefined can feel your life force energy when in your presence.

If you have this center defined, you are a generator or manifesting generator.

---

*"I allow myself to remove things that no longer make me happy so I can make space for new opportunities."*

AFFIRMATION FOR THE DEFINED SACRAL

---

Low expression of the defined sacral can look like:

- You fear you are taking up too much space by being too passionate or driven
- Your energy is depleted as you find yourself frustrated, forcing and doing things from a place of "should"
- You ignore your sacral "yes/no"
- You do not lead with desire

- You expect others to be able to do the same amount of work as you

High expression of the defined sacral can look like:

- You are continually growing and creating
- You have trust in your sacral response even when it doesn't make sense
- You release the pressure to "do do do" and allow pleasure into your life

## AN EXAMPLE OF LIVING WITH A DEFINED SACRAL

Arnaud runs a dog kennel. On his days off, he loves to walk the neighborhood dogs and volunteer at the local vet clinic. Arnaud's friends don't understand how he has so much energy to do "everything". The truth is, doing more of what Arnaud loves, creates energy for him. Arnaud has a defined sacral center.

## THE UNDEFINED SACRAL

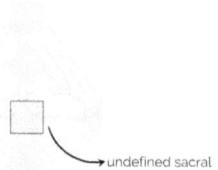
undefined sacral

34% of the population have an undefined sacral.

With an undefined sacral, you feel the buzz of energy around you through people, places and things - even the desires of others. The wisdom here is your ability to see what lights other people up, even when they are unable to see it themselves. The buzz of energy can fuel you to work hard but simultaneously, make it difficult to be aware of when to stop and rest. Your awareness to recognize when enough is enough is essential to maintain health of the body, mind and soul.

*"I honor my energy and give myself permission to rest and play."*

AFFIRMATION FOR THE UNDEFINED SACRAL

Low expression of the undefined sacral can look like:

- You are unable to hold healthy boundaries with work
- You do not know when "enough is enough"
- You may find it difficult to know when to rest
- You are overworked and exhausted

High expression of the undefined sacral can look like:

- Naturally have a calm energy
- You understand that your energy will ebb and flow
- There is harmony with your work and rest cycle

## AN EXAMPLE OF LIVING WITH AN UNDEFINED SACRAL

Nancy and Steve have been in a relationship for 5 years. Steve works in his own office with very little social interaction, mostly sitting behind a computer screen. On the weekends, Steve hangs out with Nancy and seems "normal". It drives Nancy crazy that during the week he is so tired, requiring a nap when he comes home from work.

Out of the blue, they decide to do a couple Human Design reading. They find out Steve is a projector and Nancy is a generator. Nancy begins to feel terrible for accusing Steve of having an affair. Nancy has a defined sacral and happily works in a fulfilling job. Steve has an undefined

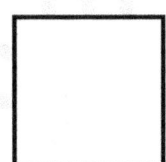

sacral, he has no defined motor centers in his bodygraph. When he is around Nancy, his undefined sacral center is fueled by the motor within Nancy's defined sacral center.

**DEFINED SACRAL**

*notes, reflections, people I know with a defined sacral*

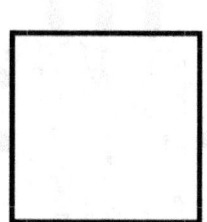

**UNDEFINED SACRAL**
*notes, reflections, people I know with an undefined sacral*

# CHAPTER 12
# THE WHISPERER

The whisperer aka the spleen, is the bottom left triangle in the bodygraph. The *spleen* is an awareness center and allows us to tap into our intuition.

## THE DEFINED SPLEEN

defined spleen

55% of the world's population have a defined spleen.

With a defined spleen, you have a deep inner knowing. You can be spontaneous, highly intuitive and the high vibration from your defined spleen can be felt by those around you. With consistent access to intuition, it is important for you to raise your awareness. The splenic hits aka 'your intuition' come moment to moment and unlike other centers, the spleen is quiet and quick. Attention to how the messages feel within your body is important as it differs person-to-person.

*"I trust my senses and understand they will guide me to keep me safe and healthy."*

AFFIRMATION FOR THE DEFINED SPLEEN

Low expression of the defined spleen can look like:

- You fear that no one will trust your intuition
- You may experience doubt and feel regret for not trusting your instincts
- You find yourself in a repeat state of your not-self theme

High expression of the defined spleen can look like:

- You have strong instincts
- You are deeply connected to your intuitive hits
- You can dissever yes and no
- You understand what feels good vs unsafe

## AN EXAMPLE OF LIVING WITH A DEFINED SPLEEN

Hendrix has a small group of friends that have nicknamed him, "Godspeed". For as long as they can remember, he always knows the answer. Hendrix easily became the "go-to" guy in their friend-group. If you don't know whether to go left or right? *Ask Hendrix*. Unsure if you should visit your friend in the hospital tomorrow? *Ask Hendrix*. When Hendrix is asked how he knows, he states, "I just know". Hendrix has a defined spleen and never questions his inner whisper. Though he doesn't understand how he knows the answers, he has built an unwavering relationship in trusting his intuition and allows that to guide him.

## THE UNDEFINED SPLEEN

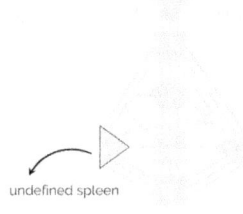
undefined spleen

45% of the population have an undefined spleen.

• • •

With an undefined spleen, your safety is often felt from others. The safety you feel can prevent you from letting go of people and things that are unhealthy for you. You may also find you are feeling the fear of others and take it on yourself - as if it is being mirrored back to you (because, it is). It is important for you to learn what is healthy for you and be able to recognize what feels right and what does not. Grounding yourself in nature, breath or movement can bring clarity when you feel uneasy and overwhelmed.

---

*"I am strong and independent. I do not need others to feel secure."*

AFFIRMATION FOR THE UNDEFINED SPLEEN

---

Low expression of the undefined spleen can look like:

- You may find yourself dependent on others
- You may hold onto relationships or jobs (even when unhappy) as they make you feel a false sense of security
- You are overly spontaneous
- You fear change

UNDERSTANDING HUMAN DESIGN CENTERS   79

High expression of the undefined spleen can look like:

- Heightened awareness to illness or danger
- You allow yourself to feel fear and understand why it is there
- You release energetic attachment to people, places, things

## AN EXAMPLE OF LIVING WITH AN UNDEFINED SPLEEN

Maya is 22yrs old and studies social sciences at a nearby University. Maya did not leave home for University so she could stay close to her parents. Maya lives in her parents basement. She has been dating the same guy since high school but their relationship has been rocky. He tends to have a temper and like Maya, he also lives at home with his parents.

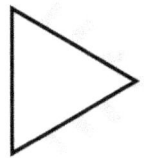

Since coming to University, Maya has made new friends. These new friends always ask, "why are you with your boyfriend?" Maya usually shrugs her shoulders and doesn't give it much thought.

One night after fighting over something silly with her boyfriend, Maya goes to bed angry. She begins to think about what her friends have been saying, wondering why she has stayed in such an unhealthy relationship. To Maya, the relationship felt 'comfortable', giving her a sense of security even though it did not make her happy. Maya has an undefined spleen.

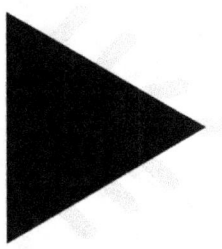

**DEFINED SPLEEN**
*notes, reflections, people I know with a defined spleen*

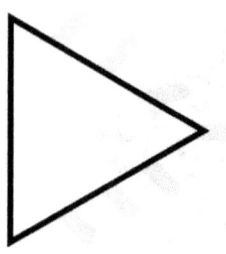

**UNDEFINED SPLEEN**
*notes, reflections, people I know with an undefined spleen*

---

# CHAPTER 13
# THE CAFFEINATOR

The caffeinator aka root center, is the final square within the bodygraph. The *root* is a pressure and motor center and is for stress and adrenaline.

## THE DEFINED ROOT

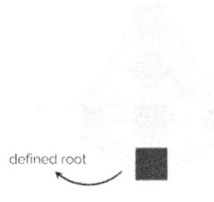

60% of the population have a defined root.

With a defined root, you can handle stress and pressure well. When you follow your strategy and authority, you do not rush or put pressure on others, you are able to utilize this pressure center to stabilize yourself and others in situations of high stress. You are capable of handling anything, even when in the eye of a storm. Under times of high pressure, you have the capacity to stay calm and thrive on intense energy instead of feeling more stress. Since you are able to handle the stress of completing things last minute, you may find you "procrastinate". This  procrastination can cause someone with an undefined root to feel overwhelmed as it is unhealthy for them to hold adrenaline within their body.

*"My access to momentum is a gift. I allow myself to rest and refuel energetically."*

AFFIRMATION FOR THE DEFINED ROOT

Low expression of the defined root can look like

- You feel you are slow completely tasks (you like speed)
- You feel pressure constantly
- You may find you are projecting your stress onto others and become angry, bitter, frustrated, disappointed or overbearing.

High expression of the defined root look like:

- You understand everyone handles pressure differently
- You have stability in the way you move through high-pressure situations
- You release stress in a healthy way

## AN EXAMPLE OF LIVING WITH A DEFINED ROOT

Ryan and Jordan have been married for 5 years. Each time they go on vacation Ryan packs last minute, it drives Jordan crazy. Ryan doesn't understand how his actions can bother Jordan so much. Jordan explains to Ryan that his procrastination causes him anxiety because he feels he's going to forget things or make them late - neither of which have happened. Ryan thrives under pressure though understands how this can cause Jordan to feel uncomfortable. Ryan has a defined root. Jordan has an undefined root.

## THE UNDEFINED ROOT

40% of the population have an undefined root.

With an undefined root, you do not produce your own energy from this center - you feel adrenaline by absorbing it from others. This can make you a "thrill-seeker" as you crave the burst of adrenaline as it fuels the body.

When you follow your strategy + authority you still have the ability to work fast and under pressure. When you do not, you can feel exhausted and stressed - remember, it is not sustainable to feel pressure constantly. You are meant to hold it temporarily and then, release it. The wisdom lies within your awareness - to be in stillness when feeling overwhelmed or moving the energy through your body through activity, etc.

---

*"I am meant to feel adrenaline in bursts. I give myself permission to release the pressure others project onto me."*

AFFIRMATION FOR THE UNDEFINED ROOT

---

Low expression of the undefined root can look like:

- You feel pressure to get things done, which can cause a feeling of "going in circles"
- You rush tasks so you can rest
- You may feel stuck or "frozen" when high stress situations arise
- You set unrealistic goals for yourself

High expression of the undefined root can look like:

- You understand there is no need to rush
- You take time to complete tasks, detaching from the need to finish under set deadlines
- You allow the adrenaline to fuel you instead of creating a negative feedback loop of overwhelm

## AN EXAMPLE OF LIVING WITH AN UNDEFINED ROOT

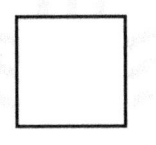

Howie has an undefined root. The pressure from the root center feels suffocating at work. His work environment is co-working, meaning people are around his work-space often. To Howie, it seems his co-workers are always checking off tasks, whereas Howie seems to never get things done. He feels distracted and annoyed being in the office.

. . .

When Howie learns about his Human Design centers, he asks his boss if he can move his deck to face a wall to limit his distractions. Howie now set's timelines for himself in a healthy way and at times, puts in his headphones so he is unable to hear other people speaking about completely their work. He notices by making these small changes, the pressure he feels is much less and he can work at his own pace with more ease.

# UNDERSTANDING HUMAN DESIGN CENTERS

**DEFINED ROOT**
*notes, reflections, people I know with a defined root*

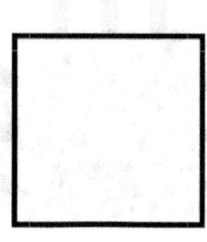

UNDEFINED ROOT

*notes, reflections, people I know with an undefined root*

# CHAPTER 14
# UNFOLDING

After doing Human Design readings for hundreds of souls, the question I get asked most is, *what now?*

With any change, the first step is to deepen your awareness. It's time to become aware of your behavior and spoiler alert, you've already built awareness by reading this book.

My suggestion is to come back to this information frequently and time-after-time, use self-reflection. Begin noting examples from your life in the low and high expressions, allowing it to hit differently with each read. Re-reading allows your subconscious to anchor in the learning and with time, unlearn the conditioning held within the centers. When you feel yourself in the low expression of a center, ask yourself, "how can I shift my energy?" At times, a shift in energy can be moving your body, changing your environment, or allowing yourself to feel an emotion in order to move past it.

. . .

And this, is where the great unfolding begins. You learn new ways of responding versus reacting and you create new patterns for yourself. Patterns that hold more compassion for who you are and who you are becoming.

Always, always, come back to what feels good for you. Our centers and any aspect of Human Design are here to illuminate who we are designed to be, *not* hold us back. If something doesn't resonate, simply leave it behind and move forward.

Sending love and grace as you uncover your uniqueness.

— Lisa

PS. As you align your energy to your uniqueness, your Human Design, you put yourself in an priceless position to inspire someone else.

Simply by leaving your honest opinion of this book on Amazon, you'll show new readers where they can find information to begin understanding their true self.

Thank you so much for spreading the word. Your bravery to heal and know yourself is what will now inspire someone else to do the same.

>>> Click here to leave your review on Amazon.

# RESOURCES

Chetan Parkyn, C. P. (2010). *Human Design: Discover the Person You Were Born to Be.* New World Library.

Ha, Bunnell, R. H. L. B. (2011). *Human Design: The Definitive Book of Human Design, The Science of Differentiation.* HDC Publishing.

Human Design Hawaii. (n.d.). *Human Design: The 9 Energy Centers.* Retrieved July 6, 2022, from https://humandesignhawaii.com/hd-basic/9-centers/

Human Design Tools. (n.d.). *9 Human Design Energy Centers.* Retrieved July 6, 2022, from https://humandesigntools.com/2019/01/31/human-design-centers/amp/

Jovian Archive. (n.d.). *The Nine Centers.* JovianArchive.Com. https://www.jovianarchive.com/Human_Design/The_Chart_and_BodyGraph/Centers

Manifesting Human Design. (2022, May 9). *9 Human Design Centers – An Overview Of The Fascinating System.* Retrieved June 7, 2022, from https://manifestinghumandesign.com/human-design-center/

Projector Movement. (2020, December 22). *How To Read Your Human Design Chart | Step By Step Guide.*
https://www.projectormovement.com/blog/how-to-read-your-human-design-chart

Pure Generators. (n.d.). *Pure Generators Blog.* Retrieved July 6, 2022, from https://www.puregenerators.com/blog

Sort of Spiritual. (2020, April 24). *Human Design Energy Centers* [Video]. YouTube. https://www.youtube.com/watch?v=1e88X5I-Z54&t=374s

Wisdom Keepers. (n.d.). *The Open Centers.* https://www.wisdomkeepers.net/the-open-centers.html

www.ingramcontent.com/pod-product-compliance
Lightning Source LLC
Chambersburg PA
CBHW071402080526
44587CB00017B/3159